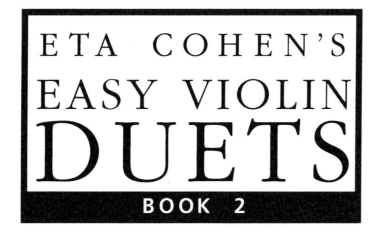

ETA COHEN'S
EASY VIOLIN
DUETS
BOOK 2

Written and arranged by Christine Brown
Edited by Eta Cohen

Novello Publishing Limited

Order No. NOV916185
ISBN 0-85360-762-1
© Copyright 1997 Novello & Company Limited

Music set by Stave Origination.
Cover design by xheight design Limited.

CONTENTS

FOREWORD

The duets in Book 2 gradually increase in difficulty: more advanced keys and rhythms are introduced and the musical demands are greater. The score format is used to encourage players to be aware of both parts. The duets cover a wide range of styles and introduce pupils to the music of different periods and countries.

The two parts are of equal difficulty and the main melodies are shared between the players so that the parts are of equal interest. The fingerings are suggestions only; different fingerings may be used at the teacher's discretion.

These duets, which can be studied in conjunction with ETA COHEN'S VIOLIN METHOD books 1 and 2, or with any other violin tutor, will provide additional repertoire and useful sight-reading practice. Above all, they will give players the great pleasure of making music together.

Eta Cohen & Christine Brown

1 THE CARRION CROW

Play crisply with fairly short strokes at the middle of the bow.

English traditional
Arr. Christine Brown

2 THE LITTLE DOVE

Play this tenderly with very smooth bows.

Czech Folk Song
Arr. Christine Brown

3 SHEPHERDS, REJOICE

Play very joyfully with firm rhythm and using fairly short bows.
Observe all the slurs.

French Traditional Carol
Arr. Christine Brown

4 THE SAILOR BOY

This is a very lively dance. Play the
melody firmly and keep the quavers light.

English Traditional Song
Arr. Christine Brown

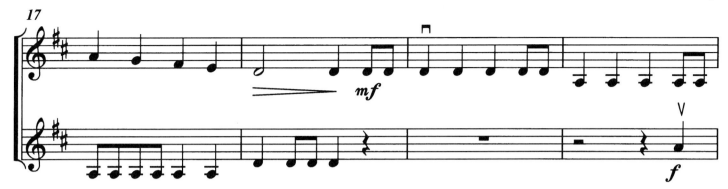

5 WIDE THE DANUBE FLOWS

Keep this flowing like the river. Your wrist
should be supple when crossing the strings.

Hungarian Folk Song
Arr. Christine Brown

* **Keep the first finger firmly on both strings to play this passage.**

** **Keep the second finger firmly on both strings to play this passage.**

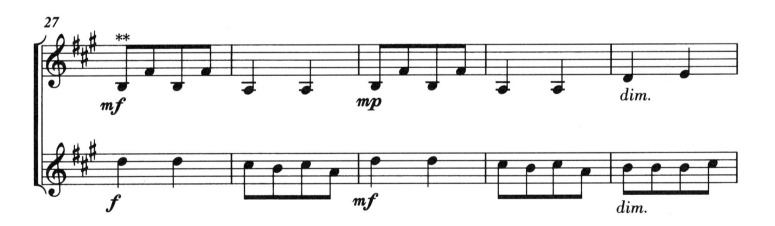

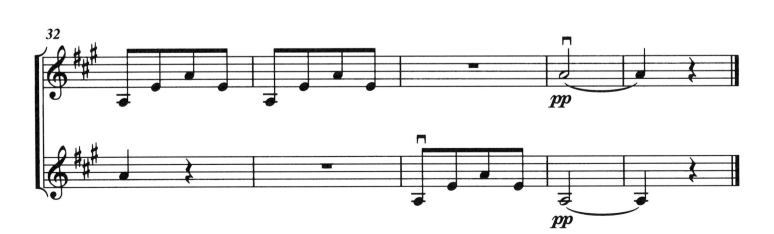

6 BOOTS OF SHINING LEATHER

This is a very lively piece.
Use fairly short bows and observe the dynamics.

Hungarian Round
Arr. Christine Brown

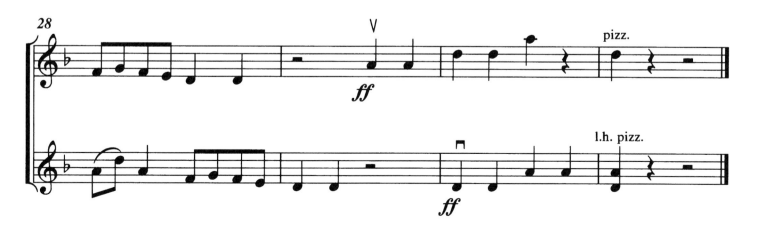

7 MINUET

A minuet is a stately dance.
Where there is a crotchet with a dot above it
lift the bow off the string and put it back gently.

G.P. Telemann
Arr. Christine Brown

Tempo di menuetto

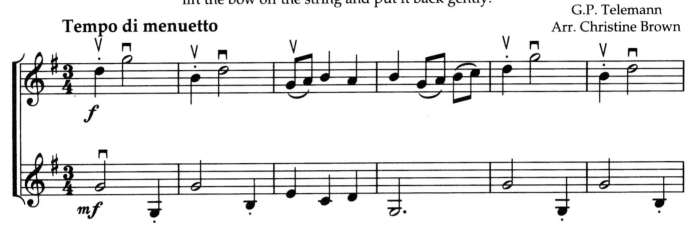

16

8 THE HANDSOME BUTCHER

Play this with vigour. Keep your wrist loose when playing the quavers
and be sure to observe the dynamics.

Hungarian Folk Song
Arr. Christine Brown

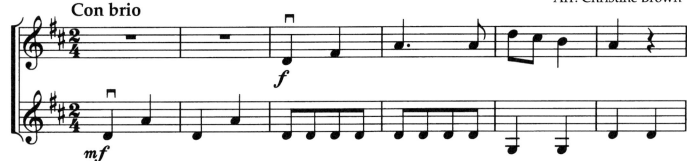

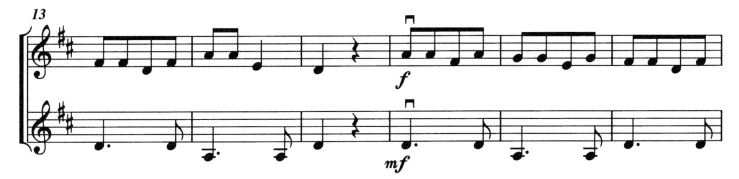

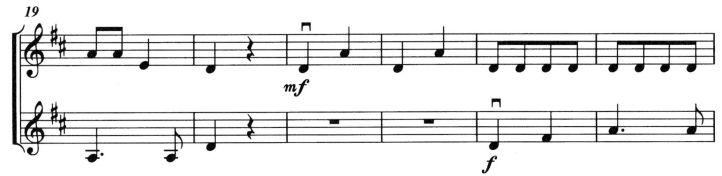

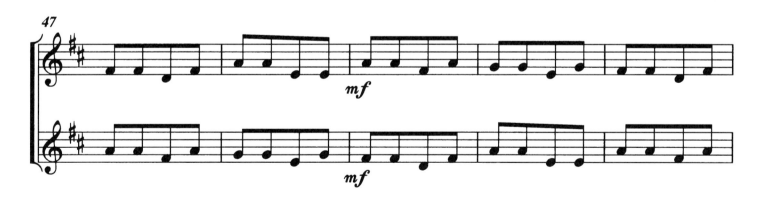

9 AS I WAS A-WALKING

Imagine you are strolling in the
country on a spring morning.

English Traditional
Arr. Christine Brown

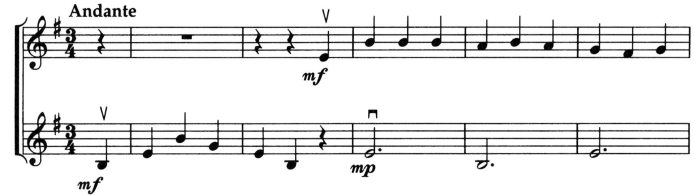

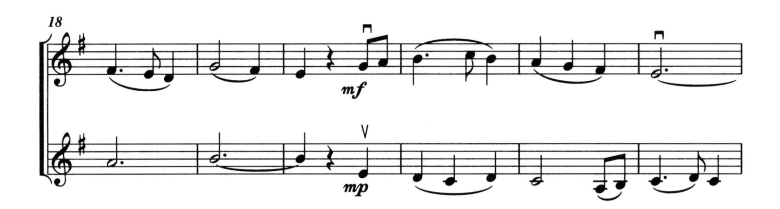

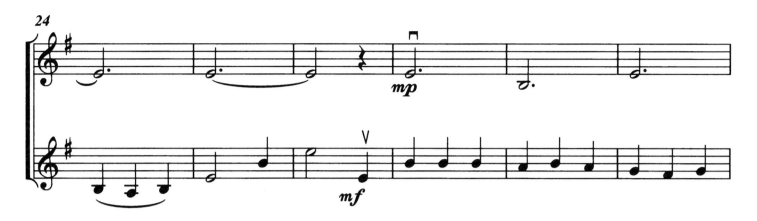

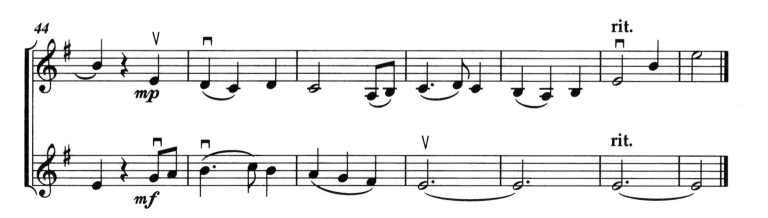

10 RIDING ON MY CHARGER

Play vigorously with firm strokes at the middle of the bow
and keep your wrist flexible. Lift the bow for the quaver rests.

German Folk Song
Arr. Christine Brown

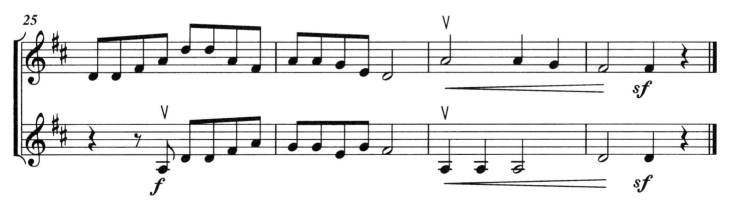

11 BOURRÉE

Play this dance at a brisk pace feeling two beats in a bar.
The crotchets could be played with martelé bowing.

C. Graupner
Arr. Christine Brown

12 COUNTRY GARDENS

This should be very carefree — think of a sunny summer's day.
Keep the rhythm crisp.

Traditional English Dance Tune
Arr. Christine Brown

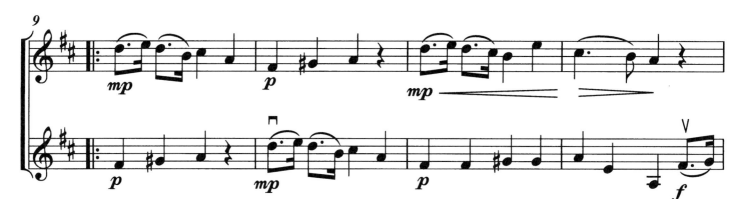